DATE DUE

AUG 1 4 1998		
OCT 0 2 1998		
OCT 3 2 1998		
OCT 0 3 1998		

FIRST LOOK AT

THE

AIRPORT

For a free color catalog describing Gareth Stevens' list of high-quality children's books, call 1-800-341-3569 (USA) or 1-800-461-9120 (Canada).

Library of Congress Cataloging-in-Publication Data

Butler, Daphne, 1945-
   [At the airport]
   First look at the airport / Daphne Butler.
      p. cm. -- (First look)
   Previously published as: At the airport. c1990.
   Includes bibliographical references and index.
   Summary: A simple introduction to airports and the many activities
that take place there.
   ISBN 0-8368-0501-1
   1. Airports--Juvenile literature. [1. Airports.] I. Title. II. Series: Butler,
Daphne, 1945- First look.
TL725.B87 1991
387.7'36--dc20   90-10266

North American edition first published in 1991 by

Gareth Stevens Children's Books
1555 North RiverCenter Drive, Suite 201
Milwaukee, WI 53212, USA

Photograph credits: Gatwick Airport Ltd.,16, 18, 19; Quadrant, 9, 25; Singapore Airlines, 17; Telegraph Colour Library, 6, 7; ZEFA, cover, 11, 13, 14, 21, 23, 24, 26, 27, 28, 29

Series editor: Rita Reitci
Design: M&M Design Partnership
Cover design: Laurie Shock

Printed in the United States of America

1 2 3 4 5 6 7 8 9 97 96 95 94 93 92 91

FIRST LOOK AT

THE AIRPORT

DAPHNE BUTLER

Gareth Stevens Children's Books
MILWAUKEE

Books in the
FIRST LOOK series:

CONTENTS

WATCHING PLANES

Have you ever watched planes landing at an airport? Do you remember the deafening roar of the engines?

How do the planes know where to land? And how do they know which way to go afterward?

"CAN WE LAND, PLEASE?"

This is the inside of the control tower at an airport. The control tower is up high so the controllers can see all around the airport.

Pilots talk to the controllers on their radios to ask permission to land.

9

PARKING

Once on the ground, a plane taxis around the airport to its parking place.

The pilot needs help to stop in just the right place. The ground crew is waiting.

GETTING OFF

The ground crew pushes the steps up to the door of the plane. The passengers start to get off.

Have you ever traveled by plane? Were the engines still running when you got off? Could you feel the wind from the engines?

13

14

TO THE TERMINAL

It's a long way from the plane to the terminal building. Do you think there will be a bus?

These passengers only have small bags to carry. The rest of their baggage is still on the plane.

PICKING UP THE BAGGAGE

Inside the terminal building, there is another long walk to the baggage claim area.

Can you see the baggage on the carousel? How do you think it got from the plane to the baggage claim area?

AT THE CHECK-IN DESK

More passengers are waiting to get on the empty planes.

First they must go to the check-in desk and reserve their seats. The computer makes a list. Then the passengers must hand in their baggage.

19

WAITING FOR THE PLANES

Now the passengers must wait until the planes are ready. Perhaps they will read books or look at the shops.

Where do you think their baggage is now?

21

GETTING THE PLANE READY

The ground crew is very busy.

The baggage carts bring the baggage. Is this the right plane? How can they be sure?

Loading the food is easy. It goes straight into the plane's kitchen!

A tanker drives up with the fuel.

Will the plane ever be ready?

23

TIME TO GO

The passengers are still waiting. They look at the departure board.

The departure board gives them directions. At last it's time for takeoff!

LAST-MINUTE CHECKS

While the passengers find their seats, the pilot is in the cockpit checking the controls.

In the control tower, the radar screen shows where other planes are in the sky.

CLEARED FOR TAKEOFF!

At last the control tower tells the pilot that it is safe to take off.

The plane taxis to the end of the takeoff runway. Then it turns around, speeds up, and thunders up, up, up into the sky.

More Books about Airports and Flying

Airlines. Petty (Franklin Watts)
Airplanes. Peterson (Childrens Press)
The Airport. Dupasquier (Putnam Publishing Group)
Airports. Jay and Hewish (Franklin Watts)
Airports. Peterson (Childrens Press)
Flying. Crews (Greenwillow)
Flying. Gibbons (Holiday)
Going on an Airplane. Rogers (Putnam Publishing Group)
In the Air. Booth (Raintree)
On a Plane. Petty (Franklin Watts)
Up in the Air. Livingston (Holiday)
What's It Like to Be an Airline Pilot. Bauer (Troll)

Glossary

Carousel: A moving belt in an airport that carries baggage around in a circle. Passengers can pick up their baggage from it.

Check-in desk: The desk where passengers go to reserve a seat on the plane. They hand in their baggage so it can be loaded onto the plane.

Cockpit: A small room at the front of the plane that has the controls for flying. The pilot and crew fly the plane from the cockpit.

Control tower: A room with big windows high above the ground. It contains radios and radar screens. The control tower lets the controllers see all the planes flying near or landed at the airport.

Controllers: People who tell the pilots where to fly so they don't get in the way of other planes. They also tell the pilots when to land or take off.

Departure board: A big board in the terminal building that tells when the planes are taking off. It also tells the passengers what gate to use to get on their plane. The arrival board tells when planes are coming in.

Ground crew: A group of people that takes care of the plane while it is on the ground. They fix anything that needs to be repaired. They also load the baggage and supplies and get the plane ready for the next flight.

Radar screen: An electronic screen in the control tower that shows signals of all the planes that are approaching or flying away from the airport. This is how controllers know where the planes are when they cannot see the planes from the control tower.

Runway: A big concrete strip where airplanes can land and take off. A busy airport has many runways and airplanes that land and take off all the time.

Taxi: To move slowly along the ground. Planes use their engines to taxi to their place after landing or before takeoff.

Terminal: The building where people go to get on a plane. They can also buy their tickets here, check in their baggage, and buy food or something to read while they wait.

Index

A **boldface** number means that the page has a picture of the subject on it.